The *Scottish Food* Bible

The
Scottish Food
Bible

Claire Macdonald

BIRLINN

First published in 2014 by
Birlinn Limited
West Newington House
10 Newington Road
Edinburgh
EH9 1QS

www.birlinn.co.uk

Reprinted 2016, 2017, 2018, 2019

ISBN: 978 1 78027 228 3

British Library Cataloguing-in-Publication Data

A catalogue record for this book is available from
the British Library

Typeset by Mark Blackadder

Printed and bound by Bell & Bain Ltd, Glasgow

Contents

PINHEAD OATMEAL

Introduction

I would say the best food in the world comes from Scotland, and these days the prefix 'Scottish' before produce is synonymous with the very best quality. To any sceptics, I ask them to stop and consider for a moment the wide variety of foods produced in Scotland. The best meat to be found anywhere in the world is that from Scotland: the five native beef breeds – Aberdeen Angus, Highland, Longhorn, Shorthorn and Galloway – are all slow maturing and give the most sublimely delicious beef. Scottish lamb and pork is every bit as good. Game from Scotland cannot fill the demand for it, not only at home but throughout mainland Europe too. Fish and shellfish from Scotland knocks spots off that from anywhere else in the world. Then there's the dairy produce, which includes delicious milk, cream and yoghurt but also a wide variety of wonderful cheeses made from cows', sheep's and goats' milk, whether soft

and creamy, blue-veined, or hard cheddar-style cheeses. Scottish soft fruits – especially raspberries and strawberries, but also increasingly blueberries – are renowned the world over. Vegetables too – particularly Scottish potatoes, my favourite being the Rooster variety.

Scotland is full of food entrepreneurs. These people, from the length and breadth of mainland Scotland as well as the islands, take our incredible produce and make innovative recipes and foods, whether by taking dairy produce a step further into top-quality ice creams, or making biscuits both savoury and sweet, jams made from our wonderful fruit harvest, or smoked meat, fish and cheese. And I think that the most impressive aspect of farming and food production throughout Scotland is that, for the most part, they stem from family businesses. For example there's the Mackie clan in Aberdeenshire, who not only farm extensively but also make potato crisps and sumptuous ice cream. Then there's the Graham family of dairy producers, now in their third generation, from Bridge of Allan, while the best known haggis makers are the legendary Macsweens, also in their third generation, who hail originally from the north end of Skye. These are just a few examples, but from cheese producers to livestock farmers, fish merchants to smokers, there are many, many more families I could cite.

This little book contains a collection of recipes which are not necessarily traditional, but which each reflect all that is so good about the food produced in Scotland. Some of the recipes are my own interpretations of classics – for example Cullen skink, which I renamed creamy smoked haddock soup and which I think is greatly improved by the inclusion of diced skinned and deseeded tomatoes and some chopped parsley. In another example I have taken a liberty by including grated apples in the batter for pancakes (or drop scones) and made a cinnamon butter to serve with them. So my own cooking and tasting is what drives the content of this little book.

One last note. I should state from the outset that I am not Scottish; my origins are mostly Lancashire with a dollop of Geordie. I have, however, been married to a Scot – very much a *Sgitheanach* (Skye native) – for almost 45 years. Therefore I speak about Scottish food dispassionately, entirely motivated by my love of eating and the sheer quality of Scottish food.

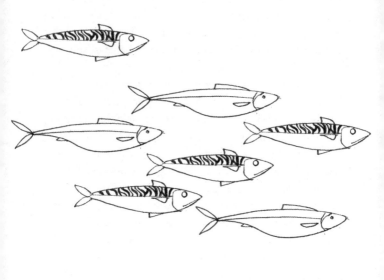

Fish and Shellfish

It is widely believed that the best fish and shellfish in the world is that caught in the waters around the Scottish coast. However, I am including only one recipe for salmon – the most famous of Scottish fish – because you will find numerous delectable salmon recipes within *The Scottish Salmon Bible*. I am also omitting lobster, because lobster too often disappoints. When lobster travels, toughening enzymes are released, too frequently completed by the lobster then being overcooked. Whereas lobster eating results in a thin wallet and increased local sales of dental floss, it is only really delicious when it is brought directly from the sea to the pot, and when it is cooked in the safe hands of our beloved Marcello Tully at Kinloch, or Andrew Fairlie at Gleneagles. *Then* lobster is the treat it should be. Here instead you will find recipes for langoustines, scallops and crab, which all tie for top place in my personal list of shellfish. Here is a taste of the superb fish and shellfish to be enjoyed throughout Scotland.

Creamy fish and shellfish chowder

This is a heavenly combination of fish and shellfish – the very essence of the best to be found in Scottish waters. It makes a very good main course because of the hearty combination of fish, shellfish and vegetables. The addition of bacon seals the deal.

Serves 6 as a main course

3 tablespoons olive oil

2 onions, skinned, halved and neatly diced

4 rashers dry-cured back bacon, the fat trimmed off with scissors, the bacon sliced into fine strips

2 leeks, washed and trimmed at either end and sliced finely

220g (8oz) Jerusalem artichokes, weighed when peeled and chopped evenly

2 bulbs fennel, trimmed at either end and halved top to base, then sliced into very fine strips

4 fairly large potatoes, peeled and sliced into thumbnail-size dice

900ml (1½ pints) vegetable stock

1 teaspoon salt

About 15 grinds of black pepper

1 teaspoon Tabasco

300ml (½ pint) double cream

450g (1lb) firm white fish such as cod or hake, trimmed of skin and bones and cut into 2cm (1") chunks

450g (1lb) monkfish fillets, cut into 2cm (1") chunks

12 langoustines, medium to large, shelled (and halved if large)

6 king scallops, the small opaque white ridge trimmed from each using scissors, and the scallops halved horizontally

2 tablespoons finely chopped parsley

In a large saucepan heat the olive oil and fry the onions for about 5 minutes, stirring occasionally, until they are transparent – don't let them colour. Scoop them out of the pan, leaving behind as much of the oil as you can. Fry the finely sliced leeks for 3–4 minutes over a moderate heat – they take less time to cook than the onions, but they mustn't be allowed to brown. Scoop them into the bowl with the onions. Fry the sliced fennel and bacon strips together for a further few minutes, then add the diced potatoes and chopped Jerusalem artichokes to the pan and fry, mixing well, for a couple of minutes.

Replace the onions and leeks in the saucepan with the potatoes, artichokes and bacon and add the stock, Tabasco, salt and pepper. Bring the liquid to a gentle simmer and cook, uncovered, until the pieces of potato are soft, and the sliced fennel feels tender when stuck with a fork – about 12–15 minutes. You can prepare the chowder to this stage up to 24 hours in advance.

Reheat to simmering point, stir in the double cream – it must be double – and when the liquid in the pan is simmering, add the fish except the langoustines. Cook, simmering gently, for about 5 minutes, stirring occasionally. A couple of minutes before serving, stir in the langoustines and finely chopped parsley. Ladle into warmed soup plates.

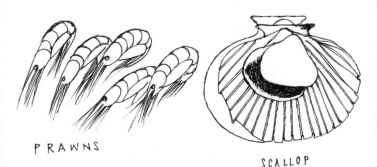

PRAWNS

SCALLOP

Creamy smoked haddock soup

This is my version of Cullen skink, the soup consisting of smoked haddock and potatoes. But I much prefer it this way, with fresh tomatoes and parsley added to it. And it is so much better when the potatoes are cooked within the soup rather than being added already cooked. Smoked haddock should never be dyed bright yellow – avoid it like the plague – but it should instead be the palest brown, hardly coloured at all. This is a filling soup and makes a wonderful main course, accompanied by chunks of bread or oatcakes and cheese.

Serves 6

675g (1½ lb) undyed smoked haddock fillets
900 ml (1½ pints) milk and water mixed
1 onion, skinned but left whole
3 tablespoons olive oil
2 onions, skinned, halved and neatly diced
3 medium potatoes, peeled and diced neatly
15 grinds of black pepper (no need for salt; the smoked haddock should contribute enough saltiness for most palates)
A grating of nutmeg
4 ripe tomatoes
1 rounded tablespoon finely chopped parsley

Feel the smoked haddock fillets on a board, and cut out any bones your fingers encounter. It is much easier to feel for bones than to look for them. Slice and pull off any skin, and cut the fish into even chunks, about 2cm (1") in size. Put these into a saucepan with the milk and water (about half milk and half water) and the skinned onion. Over a moderate heat, bring the liquid slowly to a gentle simmer and let the liquid form a skin. Take the pan off the heat and cool completely. The liquid will become infused with the flavours of the fish and onion. When cold, discard the onion, and strain the liquid into a measure jug.

To skin the tomatoes, spear each on a fork and dip it into a small saucepan of boiling water for a few seconds, then when the skin peels back from the fork tines, lift the fork and tomato out of the water, cool, then peel off the skin. Halve and quarter the tomatoes and scoop away the seeds and slice out the tiny core. Cut the tomato flesh into fingernail-sized dice

In another saucepan heat the olive oil and fry the diced onion for 4–5 minutes, stirring occasionally. Then stir in the diced potatoes and cook for a further 5 minutes, stirring from time to time. Add the reserved stock and bring to simmering point. Simmer gently, the contents of the pan seasoned with pepper and a grating of nutmeg, until the potato pieces are soft.

Using a hand-held electric blender, blitz the contents of the pan until smooth. Add the cooked pieces of smoked haddock and the diced tomatoes and reheat. Stir the finely chopped parsley through the soup just before serving.

Smoked mackerel
and horseradish pâté

Mackerel is one of the best of all fish. The fine, delicate skin belies the richness of the fish within, but they must be absolutely fresh. They are best barbecued: the flesh is so rich that there is no fear of them drying out during such a harsh form of cooking. They are an excellent source of omega 3, and when smoked they rival smoked salmon any day. Their flavour, like that of all smoked fish, is greatly enhanced by horseradish. Here is a very quick

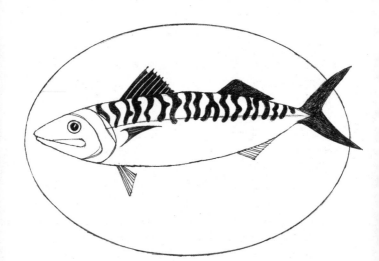

and easy pâté, useful to serve as a first course, or spooned onto mini oatcakes and served as canapés, or with crispy lettuce (e.g. little gem) as a filling for baps for a picnic.

Serves 6

4 fillets smoked mackerel

375g (12oz) reduced-fat cream cheese

2 tablespoons lemon juice

2 rounded teaspoons horseradish (I like the one made by Moniack, or by Isabella's Preserves, but Colman's is very good if you cannot source either of those)

10 grinds of black pepper (no need for salt as the smoked mackerel contributes enough)

A handful of curly parsley, without stalks

Very carefully search through each smoked mackerel fillet, removing any bones and skin. Put the fish into the food processor with the cream cheese and whiz, adding the lemon juice, horseradish and black pepper as the fish pulverises. Add the parsley just at the end – the flecks of green lift the visual appearance as well as tasting so good. Scrape the mixture from the processor into a serving bowl, cover with cling film and store in the fridge until half an hour before serving. It tastes much better after half an hour at room temperature, with the fridge chill taken off.

Smoked salmon and fried pinhead oatmeal pâté

Sumptuous smoked salmon is what I always hope pops into people's minds when the words 'Scotland' and 'food' are uttered in the same sentence. Scotland has numerous smokehouses, each giving their product its own identity. This smooth pâté has a pleasingly crunchy texture through it, thanks to the buttery fried pinhead oatmeal. Spread the pâté on oatcakes, and you double the pleasure of eating this dish.

Serves 6

220g (8oz) smoked salmon, cut into pieces
75g (3oz) pinhead oatmeal
50g (2oz) butter
Pinch of salt
220g (8oz) cream cheese (can be the reduced-fat version
    if you prefer)
1 tablespoon lemon juice
1 rounded teaspoon horseradish
About 15 grinds of black pepper

Melt the butter in a frying or sauté pan and, over a moderately high heat, fry the pinhead oatmeal with the pinch of salt, stirring occasionally, until the oatmeal is golden brown. Set aside to cool.

Put the smoked salmon into a food processor with the lemon juice, horseradish and black pepper. Whiz till smooth, then add the cream cheese and whiz again until combined. Scrape this out of the processor into a bowl, and mix in the cooled pinhead oatmeal, mixing thoroughly. Scrape into a serving bowl, cover with cling film and store the bowl in the fridge until half an hour before serving.

Prawn cocktail

The best prawns in the world are langoustines. We see so many different species of prawn for sale in supermarkets and fish shops, but only langoustines, caught off the west coast of Scotland, have the sweet succulence so lacking in every other type of prawn. I can never make up my mind which is the worst: the pink commas, usually sold frozen which taste of nothing at all, or the larger grey tiger prawns flown in from Bangladesh, which turn pink when cooked, but which only taste of whatever sauce accompanies them. Langoustines, on the other hand, fulfil every hope in terms of both flavour and texture – providing, that is, that they are properly cooked.

This prawn cocktail is a very retro but extremely popular first course. Use either fat tumblers or cocktail glasses, and fill them one third full with finely sliced little gem lettuce. Allow 4–6 langoustines per person, depending on their size, and cut large ones into half or three, but keep 6 langoustines whole, for garnishing by draping one over the rim of each glass. For this it is best to cool the cooked langoustines curled up. When it comes to the sauce, do try to banish the words 'Marie' and 'Rose' from your thoughts. This is so much nicer.

Serves 6

4–6 cooked langoustines per person
4 level tablespoons crème fraiche
2 tablespoons good (preferably homemade) mayonnaise
1 tablespoon Worcester sauce
1 tablespoon lemon juice
1 teaspoon Tabasco
1 teaspoon salt
About 12 grinds of black pepper
6 pinches of cayenne pepper – one for each prawn cocktail

Mix together the ingredients for the sauce, and fold in the halved or thirded langoustines. Divide this mixture evenly between the 6 glasses. Dust the surface of each with a pinch of cayenne pepper. Drape a whole, shelled langoustine over the rim of each glass. Serve with oatcakes or brown bread and butter.

How to cook langoustines: Have a large, wide and fairly shallow pan of simmering water. Put in no more than 6 langoustines at a time, and count slowly to 45, then remove them with a slotted spoon, to cool on large plastic trays, flattening the langoustines so that they cool straight, instead of curled up. Beware cooking too many at once; they are so much better cooked in relays. And never pile them up to cool, as they will continue to cook. They cool quickly, and can then be piled up.

Smoked haddock fishcakes

Fishcakes are positively deadly when made with unsmoked fish – even ritzy-sounding salmon fishcakes are a disappointingly bland combination of fish and mashed potatoes. Yet a good fishcake is food for the gods, and can form the perfect meal whether for breakfast, lunch, high tea or supper. I do like to serve fishcakes with crispy streaky bacon – dry cured, of course. And fishcakes are convenient because they can be made 24 hours in advance of cooking.

Serves 6, allowing 2 fishcakes per person

675g (1½lb) undyed smoked haddock fillets

600ml (1 pint) milk

900g (1lb) potatoes, peeled, halved and boiled in salted water
    until tender, drained and steamed dry then thoroughly mashed

About 15 grinds of black pepper

A good grating of nutmeg

1 large egg, beaten on a plate

120g (4oz) fresh white breadcrumbs containing 1 rounded
    tablespoon finely chopped parsley – for coating the fishcakes

Olive oil, for frying (you need only a couple of tablespoons
    if you fry in a non-stick sauté pan)

Feel the smoked haddock fillets on a board and cut out any rows of tiny bones your fingers encounter. Remove any skin and cut the fish into small chunks, about 1cm (½") in size. Put these into a saucepan with the milk, cover the pan and cook over a moderate heat until a skin forms on the milk in the pan. Take off the heat and cool completely.

Strain about a quarter of the milk from the pan into the mashed potatoes and beat well with a wooden spoon.

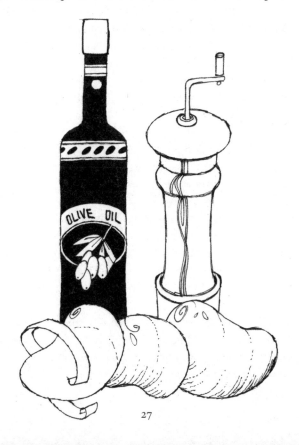

Beat in the black pepper and nutmeg. Strain off the rest of the cooking milk down the sink, and tip the cooked smoked haddock into the mashed potatoes. Mix very well.

Put a sheet of baking parchment onto a large plastic tray. Dampen your hands and form the smoked haddock and potato mixture into even-sized balls. Put them onto the parchment-lined tray and, with the palm of your hand, flatten each into a cake shape. Dip each cake in beaten egg then into the parsley crumbs and replace on the parchment. Leave in a cool place until you are ready to cook.

Heat 2 or 3 tablespoons of olive oil in a wide non-stick sauté pan. Put the fishcakes into this, well spaced, and cook over a moderately high heat. Try to resist the temptation to push the fishcakes around within the pan; leave them alone as they are frying, and this way each fishcake will fry to golden crisp within about 90 seconds. Then turn over each fishcake and cook on the other side for the same time. As they are cooked, lift them onto a warm dish lined with a couple of thicknesses of absorbent kitchen paper and keep them warm till you are ready to serve.

These are good with any green vegetable, but I love them with steamed purple sprouting broccoli – and, for a special occasion, with hollandaise sauce. At other times, tomato ketchup is a must in our house, but only that made by Heinz.

Herring in oatmeal

The herring season (August/September time) is all too brief and we buy plenty of herring to make the most of them. This is the simplest and best way to cook and eat herring.

Serves 2
2 herrings, cleaned and gutted
175g (6oz) pinhead oatmeal
1 teaspoon salt
2–3 tablespoons of olive or rapeseed oil, for frying

Mix the pinhead oatmeal and salt together on a plate. Press each herring on either side in the oatmeal. Meanwhile, heat the oil in a wide, non-stick sauté pan over a fairly high heat. Put the coated herring into the pan and fry for a couple of minutes on either side. Serve immediately.

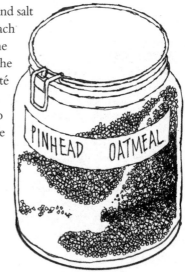

PINHEAD OATMEAL

Crab cakes

There is, for me, no better way to eat crabmeat than just as it is, in a 50/50 white and brown crabmeat combination, with buttered granary or seeded bread and a good dollop of mayonnaise. When eating crab hot, please note that the ratio of white to brown crabmeat differs from that used when eating crabmeat cold. And I hope it goes without saying that the crabmeat is only the best if it comes from Scotland. The very best dressed crab I ever ate was at the Oystercatcher in Portmahomack. This crab cake recipe was originally given to me by an American Macdonald very many years ago and it contained crushed cornflakes. I think it is definitely better without!

Serves 6

675g (1½lb) crabmeat – 450g (1lb) white and 225g (½lb) brown

120g (4oz) fresh white breadcrumbs made using a baked, not steamed loaf, no crust. (Make an extra 50–75g (2–3oz) breadcrumbs to use to coat the finished crab cakes, and whiz the second lot with a handful of parsley, no stalks)

2 rounded teaspoons English mustard

2 tablespoons Worcester sauce

1 level teaspoon salt

About 10 grinds of black pepper

1 large egg beaten on a plate

Olive or sunflower oil, for frying

Line a large plastic tray with a sheet of baking parchment. In a bowl mix the crabmeat thoroughly with the 120g (4oz) fresh breadcrumbs, mustard, Worcester sauce, salt and black pepper. Form into small, even-sized cakes. Press each lightly in the beaten egg then the parsley crumbs, on either side, and put the finished crab cakes onto the parchment-lined tray. When all the crab cakes are made, loosely cover them with cling film and put the tray in the fridge.

To fry, heat 2–3 tablespoons of oil in a large non-stick sauté pan. Fry the crab cakes, taking great care not to move them once they are put into the very hot oil – this is to allow the coating to form a golden crisp crust on one side of the cakes before turning them over. Allow at least a minute before looking to see if the crust has formed. As the crab cakes cook, lift them onto a large plate lined with 2 or 3 thicknesses of absorbent kitchen paper.

Crab cakes are filling, so a good homemade mayonnaise and a mixed leaf salad are good accompaniments.

OLIVE OIL

CHILLI FLAKES

WHITE CRAB MEAT

Crab, garlic and chilli spaghetti

This most delicious and simple, special-occasion main course calls for white crabmeat ONLY. If you include brown crabmeat too, the whole dish becomes stodgy. You can make the crabmeat mixture hours ahead of cooking the pasta, but once the spaghetti is drained, mix the crabmeat into the pasta with the pan on the heat, so as to allow the crabmeat mixture to heat through thoroughly.

Serves 6

450g (1lb) white crabmeat
6 tablespoons extra-virgin olive oil
Finely grated rind of 1 lemon
1 teaspoon salt
About 10 grinds of black pepper
½ teaspoon dried chilli flakes
1 garlic clove, skinned and very finely diced
1 rounded tablespoon very finely chopped parsley
Spaghetti: allow 50–75g (2–3oz) per person, boiled in plenty of
    salted water for about 5 minutes, then drained

Mix the crabmeat, olive oil, lemon rind, garlic, salt, black pepper, chilli and parsley together very thoroughly. Cover the bowl and keep it in the fridge until half an hour before you cook the pasta. Bring the bowl of crabmeat to room temperature for half an hour. Mix into the cooked, drained spaghetti, with the pan on a gentle heat, for a couple of minutes. Serve on warmed plates.

Langoustines in creamy shallot, white wine and saffron sauce

This is an excellent main course for a special occasion. I like to serve it with boiled basmati rice mixed with a couple of tablespoons of extra-virgin olive oil and a couple of tablespoons of finely chopped parsley.

Serves 6

5 or 6 cooked langoustines per person, shelled

3 banana shallots, skinned, halved lengthways and finely diced

300ml (½ pint) white wine (I use a Sauvignon Blanc, I think the very nicest of which is made by La Tunella, in Friuli. Open a bottle, and then drink the rest and another bottle with your friends as you eat this most divine of dishes)

450ml (¾ pint) vegetable stock

300ml (½ pint) double cream (it must be double; a lesser fat content will not thicken as it simmers)

2 pinches saffron

1 level teaspoon salt

About 12 grinds of black pepper

Put the shallots, white wine and vegetable stock into a saucepan on a moderate heat. Bring the liquid to a gentle simmer and cook, uncovered, until the shallots are completely soft and the liquid is reduced by at least two thirds. Add the saffron and double cream, and bring the contents of the saucepan back to a gentle simmer. Stir in the saffron, salt and black pepper. Simmer until the sauce thickens slightly.

Add the shelled langoustines only a minute or so before serving – the danger is that the langoustines sit for too long in the hot sauce, making them tough. If you prefer, cut each langoustine in half before adding them to the sauce.

Mussel, onion and parsley stew

Mussels grow prolifically around the coast of Scotland. If you pick your own, be sure to put the mussels into a bucket with a good couple of handfuls of oatmeal at the bottom. Fill it with fresh water. The mussels are supposed to clean themselves by ingesting the oatmeal, but they still need a good scrub and their 'beards' pulled off. Easier is to buy farmed mussels. These really are better because they grow naturally, but up ropes in deep seawater, where no tide ever goes out to expose them to air. I feel sure that everyone knows not to eat any mussel which, having been cooked, remains a closed shell – this means that the mussel was dead before it was picked. Be warned! This is a heavenly mussel stew, sustaining in every way.

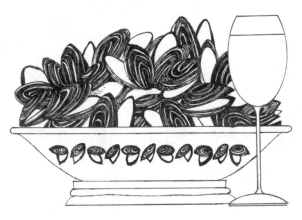

Serves 6

1.75 litres (3 pints) mussels

900ml (1½ pints) cold water

300ml (½ pint) dry white wine – my preference is for a good
    Sauvignon Blanc

50g (2oz) butter

3 onions, skinned, halved and finely diced

450g (1lb) potatoes (weighed when peeled), cut into
    thumbnail-size dice

12–15 grinds of black pepper

A grating of nutmeg

2 rounded tablespoons chopped parsley

Put the mussels into a large saucepan with the water and
white wine. Cover the pan with its lid and, over a high
heat, cook the mussels for about 6–8 minutes from when

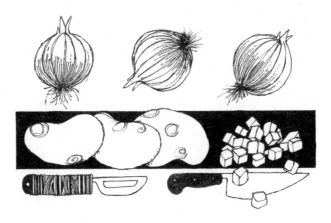

the liquid boils. Take the pan off the heat and cool. Discard any unopened mussels. When cool enough to handle, strain the cooking liquor into a large measuring jug. Take the mussels out of their shells – this is optional, but it does make for easier eating.

In a large saucepan melt the butter and fry the neatly diced onions for 5–7 minutes, stirring occasionally. Add the diced potatoes and cook for a further 3–4 minutes, stirring occasionally, then pour in the reserved liquor from cooking the mussels. Bring the liquid to a gentle simmer and simmer for about 10 minutes. The pieces of potato should feel completely soft. Season with black pepper and nutmeg and taste – add a teaspoon of salt if you think it is needed.

Add the mussels and the finely chopped parsley a couple of minutes before ladling the stew into soup plates. Beware of adding either mussels or parsley too soon: the longer they sit in heat, the tougher the mussels will become and the parsley will lose its bright fresh flavour and colour.

Scallops with chilli, cauliflower puree and crispy bacon

Scallops, the larger the better, are my absolute favourite of Scottish shellfish, along with crab and langoustines. I like to cook the coral with the white scallop meat, but stab the corals in a couple of places to help prevent them popping as they sear. When scallops are cooked over a very high heat, their surface slightly caramelises, and this maximises their delicious flavour. Scallops with black pudding are to be found on menus throughout Scotland. It is a very good combination, but one does get awfully tired of the same thing, and I like crispy cooked bacon so much more with scallops.

I first ate a spicy cauliflower puree with seared scallops at the excellent Rocpool restaurant in Inverness. Stephen Dolan, the chef/proprietor at Rocpool, is a genius of taste and flavour combinations. I have never eaten a mouthful at Rocpool which hasn't been sheer delight. This pureed cauliflower and scallop combination is his idea. The crispy bacon bits just complete the pleasure. Remember that scallops are, like all shellfish, very filling. I reckon that for a main course, 4 king scallops per person is a generous portion. For a first course, 2 king scallops are generous.

Serves 6 as a first course

For the cauliflower puree:
1 medium to large cauliflower
1 teaspoon salt
About 10 grinds of black pepper
A grating of nutmeg
½ teaspoon dried chilli flakes
Finely grated rind of 1 lemon
2 tablespoons extra-virgin olive oil
1 rounded tablespoon very finely chopped parsley

12 king scallops
4–5 tablespoons extra-virgin olive oil
About 10 grinds of black pepper
6 rashers of dry-cured streaky bacon, grilled till crisp, drained of
    excess fat on absorbent kitchen paper, then broken into
    small bits

Cut out the cauliflower's tough stalk and break the cauliflower into florets. Steam the florets until tender. Tip the
steamed cauliflower into a food processor and whiz to a
smooth puree, adding the salt, pepper, nutmeg and dried
chilli, the finely grated lemon rind and the olive oil.
Scrape the puree into a bowl and mix in the finely
chopped parsley.

Trim the small opaque ridge from the edge of each
scallop – easiest done using scissors. Stab each coral twice.
Put the scallops onto a wide plate and spoon over the
olive oil and grind the black pepper over the lot. To

cook, heat a wide sauté pan – completely dry – to a very high heat. Put the scallops into the pan, and count to 30 before flipping over each one to cook on the other side for another 30 seconds, over the same very high heat.

To assemble, place a small heap of cauliflower puree in the centre of each of 6 warmed plates, and put 2 seared king scallops on either side of the cauliflower puree. Scatter some crispy bacon bits over the top.

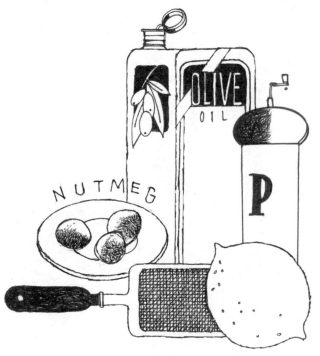

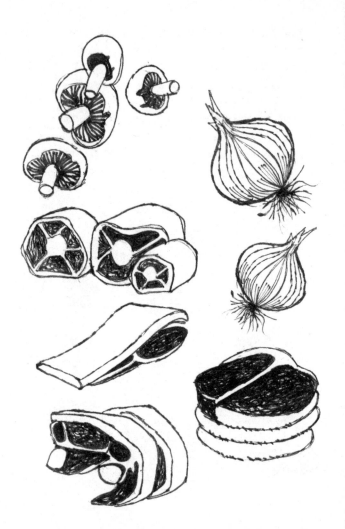

Meat

Scotland is world renowned for its top-quality beef, lamb, pork and venison. Here are some recipes using each of these wonderful meats. I have tried to vary the cuts of meat used here, to encompass the whole of the animals, including what is referred to as the '5th quarter' – i.e. offal.

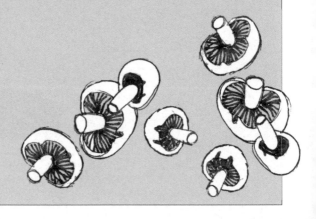

Braised lamb shanks with tomatoes and gremolata rice

This is a Scottish version of osso buco, the classic Italian dish made with veal. Scottish lamb is among the best in the world, because the meat tastes of what the animal eats – a wide range of grasses and wild herbs. Lamb shanks are inexpensive (you can pick up 4 from the excellent butcher in Dornoch for under £10) but it is important that they are from the hind legs, where there is so much more meat than the fore legs. This is one of our favourite ways to cook lamb, but lamb is the most versatile of all meats, as it is the best combined with spices, and it is good for eating all year round, whereas beef and venison really come into their own during autumn, winter and spring (unless barbecued or served cold). Just pause for a moment and think of traditional beef recipes such as steak and kidney, oxtail stew and braised brisket – all utterly delicious, but somehow so wrong to cook and eat during summer months, no matter how chilly the weather might be! This dish is so delicious with boiled basmati rice with gremolata mixed through it.

Serves 6

4 lamb shanks
3 tablespoons olive or rapeseed oil
2 onions, each skinned, halved and finely sliced
1 fat clove of garlic, skinned and diced

4 sticks of celery, trimmed at either end and peeled with a potato
    peeler (to get rid of the stringy bits) and sliced finely
3 tins (each 400g) chopped tomatoes
1 rounded teaspoon salt
About 15 grinds of black pepper

Heat the olive oil in a large casserole and brown the lamb shanks well on all sides. As they brown, remove them to a warm dish. Fry the finely sliced onions and celery, stirring occasionally, for about 5 minutes. Stir in the diced garlic and the tinned tomatoes. Stir in the salt and black pepper and, when the tomatoes reach simmering point, replace the browned lamb shanks in amongst the tomatoes, onions and celery. Cover the casserole with its lid and cook in a moderate heat (180°C / 350°F / gas 4) for 1½ hours.

Take the casserole out of the oven and cool. Before the contents of the casserole are completely cold, take up each shank and remove all the meat, discarding any bits of gristle as well as the bone. This is so much easier done whilst the lamb is just warm. When cold it tends to firm up and just takes a bit longer. Store the cooled casserole in a cold place, ideally a larder. Reheat on the top of the cooker until gently simmering, then in a moderate oven as before for 30–35 minutes from simmering.

Gremolata for rice for 6

375g (12oz) basmati rice boiled gently in salted water for 7 minutes then drained and rinsed under hot water, and drained thoroughly again.

Tip the drained rice into a warm serving dish and thoroughly mix in:
1 fat clove of garlic, skinned and very finely diced
4 tablespoons extra-virgin olive oil
2 rounded tablespoons finely chopped parsley
Finely grated rind of 1 lemon
1 level teaspoon of salt
About 10 grinds of black pepper

You can prepare the gremolata several hours in advance of cooking the rice, but store it in a covered bowl or container.

Oxtail and root vegetable stew

I think the best of *all* stews and casseroles is this one, made using oxtail. There is one vital tip to cooking oxtail: always be sure that they are fresh and not frozen. This is one cut of beef which simply does not cook properly if the meat has been frozen when raw. Cooked, the stew freezes as well (i.e. very well indeed) as any other type of meaty stew or casserole, for a fairly limited time. But then in this case, it is the root veg content that deteriorates, not the oxtail. This stew is delicious, rich and sustaining.

Serves 6

3 tablespoons olive oil

2 oxtails (cut off as much fat as you can, which is easy providing you have a really sharp knife)

2 onions, skinned, halved and finely sliced

2 fat cloves of garlic, skinned and diced

2 leeks, trimmed at either end and sliced finely

2 parsnips, peeled and trimmed at either end and sliced into little finger-thick strips

2 carrots, prepared as for the parsnips

220g (8oz) Jerusalem artichokes, peeled and chopped

1 rounded tablespoon flour

1 rounded teaspoon salt

About 15 grinds of black pepper

2 tablespoons tomato puree

600ml (1 pint) water

600ml (1 pint) lager

Heat the oil in a large casserole and brown each piece of oxtail on all sides, removing them to a warm dish as they brown. Then fry the sliced onion and sliced leeks, stirring occasionally, for 4–5 minutes. Add the rest of the prepared vegetables, stir well and cook for a further 4–5 minutes. Stir in the flour, mix well, and cook for a minute before stirring in the water, tomato puree, lager, salt and black pepper. Stir until the liquid reaches simmering point.

Replace the browned pieces of oxtail in the casserole, bring the liquid back to simmering point, cover the casserole with its lid and cook in a low heat (120°C / 250°F / gas 1) for 3–3½ hours. Cool the casserole completely. Store in a cool place, ideally a larder, for up to 2 days. To reheat, warm on top of the cooker until the gravy juice in the casserole reaches a gentle simmer then cook in a moderate heat (180°C / 350°F / gas 4) for an hour.

This is so good with well-beaten mashed potatoes and with a green vegetable, such as steamed Brussels sprouts or kale.

OXTAIL

Pork fillet stir-fried with lime, ginger, garlic and sesame

This is an excellent dish, quick to cook because all the work – not much at all – is done in the preparation. Scottish pork is so good, and our pig farmers deserve both recognition and support. This recipe illustrates the fact that Scots are now using their superlative produce, pork in this case, to combine with ingredients from around the globe. There is no need for a wok to stir-fry this dish, providing that you have a large sauté pan on a very high heat.

Serves 6

3 tablespoons olive or rapeseed oil

3 pork fillets each weighing about 375g (12oz), trimmed of any membrane, and sliced into finger-thick strips

12 spring onions, trimmed at either end, and each then cut into 3

2 cloves of garlic, peeled and diced finely

About 4cm (2") root ginger, peeled and diced finely

220g (8oz) sugarsnap peas, finely chopped (this looks better if sliced on the diagonal)

Finely grated rind and juice of 2 limes

2 tablespoons toasted sesame oil

2 tablespoons good soy sauce (e.g. Kikkoman)

12–15 grinds of black pepper (no need for salt as the soy sauce contributes enough for most palates)

2 tablespoons chopped coriander

Heat the olive oil in a large sauté pan or wok and fry the strips of pork, stirring so that they brown evenly. Scoop them into a warm bowl.

Add the sliced spring onion and sugarsnap peas, diced garlic and ginger to the pan and stir-fry for a couple of minutes, then replace the strips of pork and stir in the lime rind and juice, the soy sauce and sesame oil, black pepper and chopped coriander. Stir-fry for a further minute, then tip the contents of the pan into a warmed large bowl and serve.

Roast rack of lamb with pinhead rosemary crust

Some of the crust invariably falls off during cooking, but the oatmeal then fries in the lamb fat, and it all tastes so good!

Serves 4–5

2 racks of lamb, French trimmed, and with about half the fat sliced from them – leave a small amount

220g (8oz) pinhead oatmeal

1 rounded teaspoon salt

About 15 grinds of black pepper

A sprig of rosemary, snipped with scissors (beware using too much rosemary; the sprig should be fairly small)

Put a piece of baking parchment in the base of a roasting tin and put the lamb racks on this (the paper is there to make washing-up easier afterwards). Mix the pinhead oatmeal with the salt, pepper and rosemary and divide evenly between the two racks of lamb, pressing it over the surface as evenly as you can. Roast in a hot oven (200°C / 400°F / gas 6) for 30 minutes if you like your meat pink. Once cooked, let the racks sit, loosely covered with foil to keep in their heat. Slice between the bones to serve.

Steak and kidney pie with oatmeal crumble

I first concocted this recipe to demonstrate at the Royal Highland Show at Ingliston one year. I have been lucky enough to work with Quality Meat Scotland, doing their cooking demonstrations, at the Show for many years now. This oatmeal crumble is delicious, and healthy too – I use reduced-fat suet to mix in with the fried diced onions and the rolled oatmeal. Seasoning is vital when using oatmeal in a savoury capacity: oatmeal needs salt.

Serves 6

For the crumble:
175g (6oz) rolled (porridge) oats
2 onions, skinned, halved and finely diced
2 tablespoons olive or rapeseed oil
50g (2oz) reduced-fat suet (e.g. Atora)
1 teaspoon salt
About 10 grinds of black pepper

Heat the oil in a wide sauté pan and fry the neatly diced onions, stirring occasionally, for about 5 minutes, or until transparent. Stir in the oats, salt and black pepper. When cool, add the suet. Mix well, and set this crumble to one side (it also freezes well).

For the steak and kidney:

900g (2lb) stewing steak, trimmed of gristle and cut into
    even-sized chunks, about 2cm (1") in size

220g (8oz) ox kidney (NEVER use lambs' kidneys for this)
    cut into chunks the same size as the beef

1 rounded tablespoon flour mixed with 1 teaspoon salt and
    about 15 grinds of black pepper

3–4 tablespoons olive or rapeseed oil

1 onion, skinned, halved and neatly diced

750ml (1¼ pints) stock and red wine – I use 600ml (1 pint)
    stock to 150ml (¼ pint) red wine

Mix the seasoned flour thoroughly through the cut-up
steak and kidney. Heat the oil in a wide casserole and
brown the meats in small amounts, on all sides. Remove
the meat to a warm bowl as it browns.

Reduce the heat a bit beneath the casserole and fry
the diced onion for 4–5 minutes, until transparent. Stir in
the stock and red wine, scraping the browned bits from
the base of the casserole and stir until the liquid reaches
simmering point. Return the browned meat to the
casserole, stir well and bring the liquid back to simmering
point. Cover the casserole with its lid and cook in a
moderate oven (180°C / 350°F / gas 4) for 1 hour.

Take out of the oven and cool before spooning into
a pie dish. Place the crumble evenly over the surface. This
can all be done 24 hours in advance (loosely cover the
dish with cling film and store in the fridge). Bring to
room temperature about an hour before reheating. Put

the pie dish onto a baking tray with a sheet of baking parchment on it to make washing-up easier should any bubble over during baking. From room temperature, cook the pie in a moderate heat (180°C / 350°F / gas 4) for about 45–50 minutes until the crumble turns light brown and the steak and kidney mixture bubbles around the edges of the crumble.

Venison fillet with wild mushroom sauce

A well-hung venison fillet is a main course for a special occasion. Woods throughout the mainland and islands of Scotland are full of a variety of wild mushrooms (which should correctly be referred to as 'fungi' but I find the word fungus, or fungi in the plural, so off-putting when talking about food). At Kinloch the most prolific mushrooms are chanterelles, but we also have horns of plenty, hedgehog mushrooms and ceps galore. For this sauce, use any or a combination, or in the absence of wild, buy flat or Portobello mushrooms.

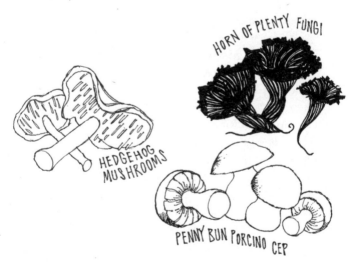

HORN OF PLENTY FUNGI

HEDGEHOG MUSHROOMS

PENNY BUN PORCINO CEP

Serves 6

For the sauce:
4 tablespoons olive oil (you may need slightly more)
3 banana shallots, each skinned and halved lengthways,
      then finely diced
900g (2lb) mushrooms, wild or otherwise, chopped
600ml (1 pint) red wine (e.g. merlot)
1 teaspoon redcurrant jelly
300ml (½ pint) double cream
1 teaspoon salt
About 15 grinds of black pepper

900g (2lb) venison fillet, any small areas of membrane
      trimmed off with a sharp knife
Olive oil
Salt and black pepper

The sauce can be made ahead and reheated. To make the
sauce, heat the olive oil in a sauté pan and fry the diced
shallots for 2–3 minutes over a moderate heat. Scoop
them into a warmed bowl, leaving behind as much oil as
you can, then turn up the heat beneath the pan and fry
the chopped mushrooms – you will need to do this in
relays, to maintain the high heat within the sauté pan. As
they fry, scoop them into the bowl with the shallots. Add
more olive oil if needed. When all the mushrooms are
well cooked, return the contents of the bowl to the sauté
pan, add the wine and simmer until it has reduced by
about two thirds. Add the double cream, redcurrant

jelly, salt and black pepper and stir until the sauce bubbles and thickens slightly.

To prepare and cook the fillet, heat the olive oil in a sauté pan with the salt and black pepper. Don't season the meat itself as this causes its juices to flow. Sear the venison fillet in the very hot seasoned olive oil, turning the fillet over and over. If you like your venison rare, then put the seared fillet onto a board, loosely cover with foil and leave to stand for 10 minutes before slicing. If you prefer your venison pink, rather than very rare, then roast the fillet for 7–10 minutes in a hot oven (220°C / 420°F / gas 7) but again, leave the meat to stand in its roasting tin, loosely covered with foil to keep it hot, for 10 minutes before slicing.

To serve, spoon the sauce over the slices of venison fillet.

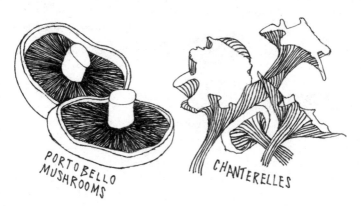

PORTOBELLO MUSHROOMS

CHANTERELLES

Turkey with lemon and onion oatmeal stuffing

Oatmeal is such a wonderful food. It feeds us, it sustains and it absorbs cholesterol. Oatmeal comes in four textures: fine, medium, coarse and pinhead, which is deliciously coarse. I use pinhead oatmeal for coating mackerel, herring and chicken fillets, as well as for this, my version of a skirlie, which I use to stuff the Christmas turkey and, on occasion, chicken or pheasant. I couldn't live without oatmeal. And for anyone living outside Scotland who finds it difficult to buy pinhead oatmeal, it is worth trying a health food store. This stuffing is for a turkey weighing approximately 6kg (12lb). You can use half the quantity to stuff 2 chickens or 2 pheasants or, if you prefer, you can bake the stuffing in a buttered gratin dish, uncovered.

---

4 tablespoons olive or rapeseed oil
3 onions, each skinned, halved and finely diced
4 sticks of celery, each trimmed at either end and very finely sliced
900g (2lb) pinhead oatmeal
2 teaspoons salt
About 20 grinds of black pepper
Finely grated rind of 3 lemons

Put the oil into a wide sauté pan and fry the diced onions, stirring occasionally, for 5–7 minutes over a moderately high heat. Then add the finely sliced celery to the fried onions in the sauté pan. Stir well and fry for a further 4–5 minutes. Scoop out of the pan into a fairly large bowl.

Put the sauté pan back on the heat and add the pinhead oatmeal to it. Stir in the salt and black pepper and fry over the same heat, stirring occasionally, for a further 4–5 minutes – this is to toast the oatmeal, and it gives it a deliciously nutty taste. Tip the toasted pinhead oatmeal into the bowl with the onions and celery, and add the finely grated lemon rind. Mix together very well. Stuff the turkey with the pinhead oatmeal stuffing, and the lemon gives a delicious flavour to the turkey fat.

Whisky and mushroom sauce

This is an excellent sauce to serve with either fish or meat. During the wild mushroom season you can substitute any wild mushrooms (correctly called fungi) for the mushroom quantity in the recipe. When you pick wild mushrooms, always take with you a clearly illustrated book to show you what is and what isn't edible. I recommend Roger Phillips' book on mushrooms, which is an excellent reference.

Serves 6

450g (1lb) mushrooms, wiped, stalks cut off, and the
      mushrooms diced into thumbnail-size pieces
2 onions, each skinned, halved and finely diced
150ml (¼ pint) whisky of your choice (I tend to use Famous Grouse)
450ml (¾ pint) stock
50g (2oz) butter + 1 tablespoon olive or rapeseed oil
1 level tablespoon flour
600ml (1 pint) milk
1 level teaspoon salt
About 10 grinds of black pepper
A good grating of nutmeg

Put the finely diced onions into a small saucepan with the whisk and stock. Over a moderate heat bring the liquid to simmering point and simmer gently until the liquid has reduced away almost completely. Stir the diced onions two or three times during the cooking. In a wide-based saucepan melt the butter and heat the olive oil until the butter is foaming. Add the diced mushrooms and cook over a high heat until the mushrooms are very well done – this intensifies their flavour. Stir in the flour, cook for a minute then stir in the milk, gradually, stirring all the time until the sauce simmers. Cook for a couple of minutes then add the contents of the whisky and stock pan, stirring the diced onions well into the mushroom sauce. Take the pan off the heat and stir in the salt, black pepper and nutmeg. The sauce can be made in advance (store it in a cold place) and reheated to serve.

64

Vegetables

I realise that vegetables have appeared in many of the preceding recipes, but there is such a wide variety of wonderful vegetables being grown throughout Scotland that they do merit a small section within this little book. I pay homage to the growers of our herbs and salad leaves in Skye, and elsewhere throughout Scotland. Scottish potatoes are some of the best to be found in the world – my favourite variety is the Rooster, which has a lovely flavour and is so good whether boiled, mashed, roasted or chipped. Winter brassicas keep us healthy, accompanied by a great variety of root vegetables. And in the summer months we have sugarsnap peas and asparagus – oh, the taste of Scottish asparagus, a different vegetable entirely from the asparagus imported from Peru. The Scottish asparagus season comes in May and the first part of June, one of our very many seasonal treats. Well worth waiting for and savouring!

Potato and leek soup

This is such an excellent soup. In this version you will see that I include a teaspoon of medium-strength curry powder – I learned this from my mother. It isn't discernible as such, but it gives a warm glow to this most comforting of soups. You can use either chicken or vegetable stock here, but my preference is for chicken.

Serves 6

3 tablespoons olive oil
1 onion, skinned, halved and chopped
3 leeks, any outer leaves removed, trimmed at either end,
    then chopped
3 medium potatoes, peeled and chopped
1 rounded teaspoon medium-strength curry powder
900ml (1½ pints) chicken or vegetable stock
1 rounded teaspoon salt
About 12 grinds of black pepper
A grating of nutmeg
6 teaspoons crème fraiche, to garnish

Heat the olive oil in a large saucepan and, over a moderately high heat, fry the onion with the chopped leeks, stirring occasionally, for about 5 minutes. Then add the chopped potatoes to the contents of the pan, stir well, and cook for a further 5 minutes, stirring from time to time to prevent sticking. Then add the curry powder and stir well. Pour in the stock, bring to a gentle simmer, season with salt, black pepper and nutmeg, and half cover the pan with its lid. Simmer gently for 8–10 minutes. Test a bit of potato to see if it is soft, then take the pan off the heat and, using a hand-held blender, blitz the contents of the saucepan until smooth. Reheat to serve, with a teaspoon of crème fraiche in the centre of each bowlful.

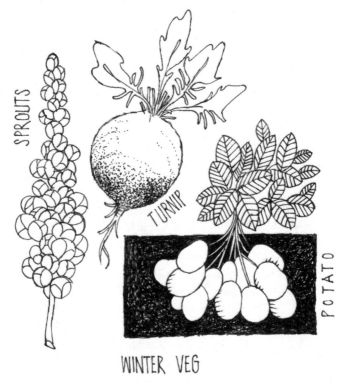

SPROUTS

TURNIP

POTATO

WINTER VEG

Mashed turnip with butter-fried seeds

I love turnip, however it is cooked. Bashed neeps are an integral part of any celebratory Burns supper, but I think that mashed turnip goes so very well with any meat or game casserole or roast. You can never get a really smooth turnip puree unless you whiz it in a food processor, but I like the fibrous texture you get by just mashing with a good potato masher. I do like a contrast of texture, and that is why I butter-fry some seeds, usually sunflower seeds, to scatter over the surface of my mashed turnip. It is of vital importance to season the turnip well, with salt, black pepper and a grating of nutmeg.

Serves 6
2 small turnips
50g (2oz) butter
1 level teaspoon salt
About 15 grinds of black pepper
A grating of nutmeg

For the seeds:
75g (3oz) seeds (either just sunflower seeds, or a combination
    of sunflower and pumpkin seeds)
25g (1oz) butter
1 level teaspoon salt

Cut the skin off the turnips with a sharp knife. Cut the turnips into even-sized chunks and put them into a saucepan. Immerse in cold water and put the pan on the heat. Bring to a simmer and cook until the turnip feels soft when stuck with a fork. Drain the turnip and steam the pan on the heat for half a minute, shaking the pan as you do so. Take the pan off the heat and mash very thoroughly. Then, with a wooden spoon, beat in the butter, salt, black pepper and grating of nutmeg.

To fry the seeds. melt the butter in a saucepan, add the salt and fry the seeds over a moderately high heat, stirring, for 4–5 minutes. The seeds should, in the case of sunflower seeds, turn pale brown. Scatter the butter-fried seeds over the surface of the mashed turnip in the serving dish.

Steamed purple sprouting broccoli with parsley breadcrumbs and capers

You can substitute tenderstem broccoli for the purple sprouting if you prefer. The parsley and caper crumbs can be prepared ahead of time and reheated before being spooned over the cooked purple sprouting, so this is a quick as well as healthy dish, useful to dress up a plain grilled or baked piece of chicken, meat or fish.

Serves 6

675g (1½ lb) purple sprouting broccoli, stems trimmed
175g (6oz) fresh white breadcrumbs mixed with
    2 rounded tablespoons chopped parsley
75g (3oz) butter
1 teaspoon salt
About 10 grinds of black pepper
2 teaspoons plump capers, drained from their brine

Steam the purple sprouting until it feels tender when stuck with a fork. Tip the steamed purple sprouting into a shallow ovenproof dish. To make the crumb, melt the butter in a sauté pan until it is very hot and foaming. Fry the parsley and breadcrumbs, salt, black pepper and capers, stirring gently to make sure that the mixture fries evenly in the butter. The crumbs and parsley should become golden brown and feel crispy. Take the pan off the heat. Cover the broccoli with the breadcrumb mixture and keep the dish warm, uncovered, in a low oven until you are ready to serve.

Cheese

I have restrained myself and restricted the cheese recipes to just four in number, yet I could fill a whole book with cheese recipes! Scotland produces the most wonderful cheeses: cows', sheep's and goats' milks, soft and creamy brie-style, blue-veined and hard cheddar-style cheeses. I believe Scottish cheeses rival (and in many cases surpass) those made in the rest of the UK and mainland Europe.

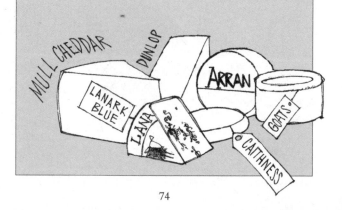

Stir-fried beetroot with shallots and orange, with grilled goats' cheese

This is a delectable combination of tastes and textures. These days beetroot are to be found in most farm shops, greengrocers and supermarkets. Beetroot is one of the best of the root vegetables available to us, not only during the autumn and winter months but also, now, during summer months too. Beetroot is so widely useful, so delicious: it can be made into thick soups, or thin soups more elegantly suitable for entertaining formally, or peeled and cut into chunks for roasting, or as in this recipe, coarsely grated and stir-fried. And beetroot grated raw in a salad is infinitely better than raw grated carrot. And beetroot contains a tenderising enzyme (as does papaya) so if you include beetroot in a meat casserole you will find that the meat takes less time to become tender than it would if cooked without beetroot!

Serves 6

4 banana shallots, each peeled, halved and neatly diced

900g (2lb) raw beetroot, weighed before peeling. Slice off either end, peel with a good potato peeler, and grate coarsely into a large, wide bowl.

3 tablespoons olive oil

Finely grated rind of 1 orange

2 teaspoons balsamic vinegar

1 teaspoon salt

About 15 grinds of black pepper

6 slices of goats' cheese

Heat the oil in a wide sauté pan, and fry the diced
shallots for about 5 minutes until soft and transparent. Stir
in the grated beetroot, raise the heat a bit and stir in the
balsamic vinegar, salt and black pepper, and grate in the
orange rind. Stir-fry for about 5 minutes – this mixture
will then keep warm in a covered dish without spoiling,
if you would like to serve it as a vegetable, and it is
particularly good with game.

To serve it as a first course, put a large metal ring on
each of 6 warmed plates and spoon into the rings as
much of the beetroot mixture as possible, pressing it
down well. Lift off the ring. Put a slice of goats' cheese
on each little tower of beetroot, and blast each with a
blow torch until the cheese is melted and the surface is
speckled golden brown.

NB: It is worth buying a good and gutsy blow torch
for this alone, but in the absence of a blow torch, you can
grill the slices of goats' cheese. Put a sheet of foil over the
grill pan. Brush it with a small amount of oil, otherwise
the cheese tends to stick to the foil. Put the slices of
goats' cheese onto the oiled foil under a hot grill, and
watch like a hawk – goats' cheese melts quicker than any
other cheese. When the slices of cheese are melting and
golden on their surfaces, take them out from under the
grill and, using a palette knife, put one slice on each
tower of grated stir-fried beetroot and serve.

Baked brie with almonds and Demerara

This sounds odd but it is simply delicious, and forms the first or main course for an informal group of friends. I buy my brie from the Connage dairy not far from where we live, on the Black Isle north of Inverness, when we aren't in Skye. Connage bries are small and are widely available throughout Scotland. Served with lots of warm, crusty bread and oatcakes, and with a side salad dressed with mustard vinaigrette, this sets the scene for a wonderful supper or lunch. Don't be put off by the thought of the Demerara; there isn't much and it is simply delicious combined with the salt and flaked almonds.

Serves 6

3 Connage bries, or any other small bries (I reckon that one feeds two people as a main course)
220g (8oz) flaked almonds
2 rounded tablespoons Demerara sugar
2 teaspoons salt
12–15 grinds of black pepper

With a sharp knife cut the top rind off each brie. Put a sheet of foil onto a baking tray, brush it with a tiny amount of oil, and put the bries onto this. In a bowl, mix together the flaked almonds, Demerara, salt and black pepper, then divide this evenly between the 3 bries, covering their entire surfaces. You can do this a couple of hours in advance of baking. Put the baking tray under a hot grill, well below the red-hot elements, and keep an eye on them as you do not want to burn the almonds, just turn them golden brown, at the same time as melting the sugar around the almonds. When the cheese is bubbling gently beneath the crust, and the flaked almonds are turning light brown, then remove the baking tray and switch off the grill. Slip the grilled bries onto a long, warmed ashet. Have baskets of chunks of warm bread and oatcakes ready on the table, along with the mustardy dressed salad, and invite your guests to dig in!

Mustard vinaigrette dressing

This dressing is so good with an assortment of salad leaves to accompany any cheese dish. A screw-topped jar of this dressing is so useful to keep on a shelf in the larder. Just give it a good stir before dressing the salad.

---

1 teaspoon caster sugar
1 teaspoon salt
About 15 grinds of black pepper
1 rounded teaspoon grain mustard (there are several excellent
    Scottish brands of mustard, my favourite possibly being that
    made by Isabella's Preserves)
2 tablespoons white wine vinegar
8 tablespoons olive oil

Mix the sugar, salt, black pepper and grain mustard together into a thick paste. Gradually add the wine vinegar, working it into the paste, then the olive oil a spoonful at a time. Pour the dressing into a screw-topped jar and store on a shelf in a cool place, ideally a larder. Mix well before spooning 3–4 tablespoons of the dressing into a mixed-leaf salad – beware using too much.

Blue cheese beignets
with tomato sauce

There are delicious Scottish blue-veined cheeses available
from several sources, but the original maker I encoun-
tered many years ago was – and remains – Humphrey
Errington. I still love his Lanark Blue. For this recipe you
can use any blue cheese that appeals to you, providing
that it is Scottish! (Do avoid Danish Blue at all costs; it
smells of ammonia and tastes of it, too.) I allow 4–6
beignets per person, and I aim to make the beignets
about the size of a walnut.

_____

Serves 6
150g (5oz) plain flour sieved onto a large sheet of baking parchment
100g (3½ oz) butter, cut into small bits
200ml (7 fl oz) cold water
120g (4oz) blue cheese crumbled or cut into small bits
3 large eggs, beaten well together
1 teaspoon of Tabasco
1 teaspoon Worcester sauce
Sunflower oil, for deep frying

_____

Put the water, Tabasco and Worcester sauce into a
saucepan over a moderate heat. Add the bits of butter to
the contents of the pan. When the butter has melted,
raise the heat beneath the pan and let the liquid come to
a rolling boil. (Don't let it boil before the butter has
melted.) Immediately add the sieved flour in one lot, and

with a wooden spoon beat the flour into the boiling buttery liquid. As soon as the dough rolls away from the sides of the pan take the pan off the heat – this will not take long. Gradually beat in the eggs; the dough will become glossy. Beat in the blue cheese and continue to beat with your wooden spoon until the cheese has melted completely.

In a deep saucepan heat the sunflower oil until, when you drop in a small cube of bread, it sizzles. Remove the bread. With 2 teaspoons drop even-sized blobs of blue cheese dough into the hot oil, and carefully turn them over as they deep fry. They will be puffed and golden brown when they are cooked, which should only take about a minute per batch of beignets. As they cook, lift them from the hot oil and drain on several thicknesses of absorbent kitchen paper on a large, warm plate. Cook further batches of beignets until the blue cheese dough is all used up. These are good served with a warm tomato sauce.

Tomato sauce

This is best made using tomatoes grown locally to where you live. Farm shops are an excellent source of these, but outwith the tomato season use tinned chopped tomatoes instead. Don't worry about the anchovies in the

ingredients: the sauce won't taste at all of fish, but it will have a depth of flavour which it lacks if you do not include the anchovies. This sauce enhances not only the Blue Cheese Beignets but each of the cheese recipes in this little book – with the sole exception of the grated beetroot stir-fried beneath the grilled goats' cheese.

Serves 6

2 onions, skinned, halved and diced finely
3 tablespoons olive or rapeseed oil
1 fat clove of garlic, skinned and diced
2 tinned anchovies, or a squeeze of anchovy paste from
    a tube (about (4cm / 2"))
2 sticks of celery, each peeled with a potato peeler to
    get rid of the stringy bits, then sliced finely
10 ripe tomatoes, halved, seeded, and chopped
    (I tend to leave the skins on)
1 teaspoon salt
About 12–15 grinds of black pepper
300ml (½ pint) vegetable stock

Heat the olive oil in large saucepan. Fry the onions, celery and garlic for 4–5 minutes, stirring occasionally. Add the anchovies (or the anchovy paste) during this time: you will find that they literally melt as they cook. Add the tomatoes, stock, salt and black pepper. Simmer the sauce over a gentle heat for 15–20 minutes. You can either serve the sauce as it is, or if you prefer a smooth sauce, you can pulverise the sauce in the saucepan, using a hand-held blender.

Three cheese tart

This is a most delicious recipe for either a starter or a main course. It is an excellent way to use up ends of cheeses, and you can use whichever cheeses appeal to you. I generally combine a brie-style cheese with some grated Isle of Mull cheddar, and either some blue-veined cheese or a semi-hard cheese, such as Loch Arthur's delicious Criffel. All that's required to enhance the flavour of this tart is a mixed-leaf salad dressed with a mustardy vinaigrette.

Serves 6

For the pastry:

120g (4oz) butter, hard from the fridge

175g (6oz) plain flour

1 level tablespoon icing sugar

1 teaspoon salt

About 10 grinds of black pepper

2 teaspoons dried pink peppercorns (optional, but very good
    in pastry with cheese)

Put the butter, flour, icing sugar, salt and black pepper into a processor and whiz to the texture of fine crumbs. Add the dried pink peppercorns (if using), but do not whizz them into the pastry crumbs; leave them whole. Press this mixture firmly over the base and up the sides of a metal flan dish measuring 22cm (9") in diameter, and put this into the fridge for at least an hour. Then bake straight from the fridge in a moderate temperature (350°F / 180°C / gas 4) for about 20 minutes – the sides will slip towards the base as it cooks, but don't worry. Using a metal teaspoon scrape them firmly back into place and bake for a further couple of minutes. Leave to cool.

For the filling:
2 large eggs beaten with a further 2 large egg yolks
300ml (½ pint) single cream
About 10 grinds of black pepper (no need for salt due to
    all the cheese)
2 teaspoons Worcester sauce
75g (3oz) Scottish hard cheese (e.g. Mull cheddar) grated
175g (6oz) brie (e.g. Connage brie) rind pared off and the
    brie cut into slivers
75g (3oz) Criffel (or any other Scottish cheese of your choice)
    rind sliced off and the cheese sliced into fine slivers

Arrange the prepared cheeses over the base of the cooled
pastry. Mix the black pepper and Worcester sauce into the
beaten eggs and yolks and mix in the single cream. Pour
this into and amongst the cheeses within the cooled
pastry, and carefully put the tart into a moderate oven
(180°C / 350°F / gas 4). Bake for about 25 minutes, until
the centre of the filling no longer wobbles. The cheeses
will have melted as the soft savoury custard sets around
them. Serve warm with a mixed-leaf salad.

Breakfasts, Puddings and Teatime Treats

The Scots have a very sweet tooth. So have I. Scottish baking is not about fine patisserie – it is entirely more robust, but oh, so delicious. Within this section there are recipes for biscuits, oatcakes, scones and pancakes, as well as some breakfast dishes to start the day well.

Porridge

Porridge brings out strong sentiments in many. It starts with the spelling. For me, it is always porridge, never porage. This recipe is how I make my porridge, and love

to eat it, but it won't be the same as the porridge made by others. Nor will theirs be the same as yet others'. So individuality is key, and you just make it like this, then adjust it to suit you. The salt is vital, though. And, for me, the milk. You may prefer using water.

Serves 2
1 breakfast cup of medium or coarse oatmeal
1 rounded teaspoon salt
2 breakfast cups of milk (I use skimmed)

Measure the ingredients into a non-stick saucepan and put it on a moderate heat. Stir, until the porridge thickens – about 5 minutes. Keep the pan on the side of the hotplate, to prevent the porridge from sticking to the base of the pan.

What you eat with your porridge is up to you, but sliced banana and a spoonful of a local honey is my ideal.

Chocolate oatmeal biscuits

These have been such a favourite with our family for over four decades. But it is the oatmeal which is the secret!

175g (6oz) soft butter
120g (4oz) caster sugar
150g (5oz) self-raising flour
25g (1oz) cocoa powder (not to be confused with drinking chocolate!)
50g (2oz) rolled oats, or porridge oats
1 teaspoon vanilla extract

Beat together the soft butter and caster sugar until pale and almost fluffy. Sieve in the flour and cocoa powder and mix well. Then mix in the porridge oats and vanilla extract, making a fairly stiff dough. Dust a work surface with flour, and flour a rolling pin. Roll out the chocolate oatmeal dough to approximately ½cm thickness. Cut into biscuits using a scone or cookie cutter, and put them onto a lightly buttered or non-stick baking tray. Bake in moderate heat (180°C / 350°F / gas 4) for 10–12 minutes. Take the tray out of the oven, wait for a minute, then carefully lift each biscuit onto a wire cooling rack using a palette knife. When cold, store the biscuits in an airtight container.

Chocolate toffee shortbread (aka millionaire's shortbread)

No book of Scottish recipes would be complete without a version of this most delectable of Scottish baked treats. This is my version. You will notice that the shortbread varies a bit from the previous recipe – this is because of the two layers that are destined to cover the shortbread.

For the shortbread:
175g (6oz) butter, softened
175g (6oz) caster sugar
220g (8oz) plain flour
50g (2oz) cornflour
1 teaspoon baking powder
25g (1oz) melted butter, for brushing the baking tray

Brush a baking tray with melted butter. Beat together the softened butter and the caster sugar. Sieve together the flour, cornflour and baking powder and beat into the butter and sugar. Press this mixture evenly over the base of the baking tray. Bake in a moderate heat (180°C / 350°F / gas 4) for 25–30 minutes or till golden brown. Cool.

For the caramel:
175g (6oz) granulated sugar
175g (6oz) butter
450g (15oz) tin of condensed milk

1 tablespoon golden syrup
1 teaspoon vanilla extract

Make the caramel by putting all the ingredients into a saucepan on a moderate heat. Stir until the butter has melted and the sugar dissolved. Bring the mixture to the boil, and boil for about 5 minutes. Take the pan off the heat and stir the contents for 2–3 minutes to cool it slightly. Then pour it over the entire surface of the cooled shortbread. Leave until cold.

For the chocolate layer:
220g (8oz) dark chocolate

Break the chocolate into bits and put in a Pyrex bowl over a saucepan containing 2cm (1") very hot (but not boiling) water. The bottom of the bowl must not touch the water. Stir the chocolate until melted, then spread over the entire surface of the cooled caramel. Leave until the chocolate is cold. Mark into squares or rectangles (beware making them too big) and store the chocolate toffee shortbread in an airtight container with a piece of baking parchment or greaseproof paper between each layer.

Optional: if you like, you can add 1 rounded teaspoon of flaked salt to the caramel when cold.

Oat flapjacks

This recipes was given to me by my greatest friend
Araminta Dallmeyer, with whom I've done cooking
demonstrations for very many years.

Makes 12

120g (4oz) butter

1 tablespoon golden syrup (dip the tablespoon into very hot water
for a minute before spooning the syrup, which will then slip
easily from the hot spoon)

120g (4oz) caster sugar

75g (3oz) porridge oats

50g (2oz) self-raising flour

50g (2oz) cornflakes

Melt the butter and golden syrup together in a fairly
large saucepan, then mix in the rest of the ingredients.
Mix well. Thoroughly butter a baking tray and tip the
mixture into this. Spread evenly, and bake in a hot oven
(400°F / 200°C / gas 6) for 15 minutes. Take the tin out
of the oven, cool for 5 minutes, then cut the flapjacks
into rectangles. When cold, store the flapjacks in an
airtight container.

Oatcakes

You can buy some delicious oatcakes made by small bakeries all around Scotland, each with their own individual quality. I think the best oatcakes are made using bacon fat – this must be fat from dry-cured bacon rashers. But we rarely get sufficient quantity of bacon fat for making into oatcakes. These are very good, and however good bought foods are, home-made is *always* better!

Makes about 30
220g (8oz) self-raising flour
450g (1lb) pinhead oatmeal
1 teaspoon bicarbonate of soda
1 teaspoon salt
150g (5oz) butter, hard from the fridge, cut into small bits
3 tablespoons milk
3 tablespoons cold water

Put the flour, bicarbonate of soda and salt into a food processor and add the cold, hard bits of butter. Whiz to the texture of fine crumbs. Then tip the contents of the processor into a bowl, and mix in the pinhead oatmeal, milk and water. Mix to a dough. Lightly dust a work surface with sieved self-raising flour. Tip out the oatmeal dough and, with a floured rolling pin, roll out to about ½cm thickness. Cut into either rounds using a scone cutter, or into even-width strips and cut these into triangles. Put the oatcakes onto a non-stick baking tray and bake in a moderate heat (180°C / 350° F/ gas 4) for about 12–15 minutes until golden brown. Remove from the oven and leave for a minute on the baking tray, then carefully lift them onto a wire cooling rack. When cold, store the oatcakes in an airtight tin. If the oatcakes are a few days old, they benefit from being laid out on a baking tray and put into the same moderate oven for 5 minutes, to refresh their flavour.

Oven scones

I have called these 'oven' scones to distinguish them from girdle (griddle) scones, or pancakes, known south of the border as drop scones, which are cooked on top of heat. (A recipe for these is further on!)

Makes about 20

700g (1½ lb) self-raising flour
1 rounded teaspoon salt
2 teaspoons caster sugar
2 rounded teaspoons baking powder
2 large eggs, beaten
2 tablespoons sunflower, rapeseed or light olive oil
300ml (½ pint) milk
150ml (¼ pint) natural yoghurt

Sieve the dry ingredients into a large mixing bowl. Beat together the eggs, oil, milk and yoghurt, then mix thoroughly into the dry ingredients – but do not overwork this mixture. Tip onto a floured work surface (the mixture will be fairly sticky) and, with floured hands, press it out to a width of about 2cm (1"). Cut out discs with a scone cutter and put them, evenly spaced, onto a floured baking sheet. Bake in a hot oven (220°C / 425°F / gas 7) for 12–15 minutes until well risen and golden brown on top. These are best made and eaten the same day.

Variations: To make cheese scones, replace 2 teaspoons of the flour with mustard powder and add 175g (6oz) grated strong cheddar cheese to the mixture. Warm cheese scones are delicious served buttered, with strawberry or raspberry jam.

Add 3 heaped tablespoons of finely chopped mixed herbs (e.g. parsley, chives and dill) to the mixture, and serve instead of bread or rolls with bowls of hot soup.

Potato scones

Tattie scones are an integral part of a breakfast fry-up, but they are delicious eaten with grilled streaky bacon alone. Oh, and for me, I would add some roasted flat mushrooms too. The potato scones cook on top of the cooker, on a griddle or in a dry frying pan.

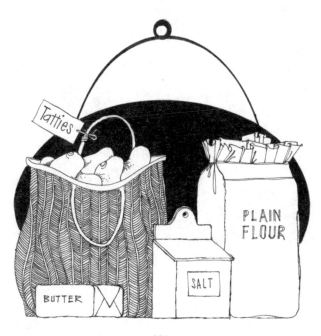

Butter

Plain
FLOUR

Salt

Tatties

Makes 10–12
450g (1lb) potatoes, weighed when peeled
50g (2oz) butter
1 rounded teaspoon salt
120g (4oz) plain flour, sieved

Boil the potatoes in plenty of salted water until tender when stuck with a knife. Drain and steam dry, then mash the potatoes very thoroughly with the butter and the teaspoon of salt. Cool. Work the sieved flour into the cooled mashed potatoes, so that you have a smooth potato dough. Lightly dust a work surface with sieved flour. Tip the potato dough onto this and roll, with a floured rolling pin, to a length about 1 cm thick, or just less. Cut this into triangles.

Heat a griddle (or dry frying or sauté pan) over a moderate heat. Put the triangles of potato dough into this and cook for 2–3 minutes on each side. They should be golden brown. Serve hot, spread with butter, which melts deliciously into the potato scones.

Shortbread

Of all the baked foods to be found in Scotland, I think
shortbread must top the list as being the best known.
There are many variations on shortbread, but this is the
one we bake at Kinloch, and have done now for over 40
years.

This fills a baking tray (non-stick) measuring 22 x
26cm (10 x 12")

450g (1lb) plain flour
220g (8oz) semolina or ground rice
220g (8oz) caster sugar
450g (1lb) butter
25g (1oz) melted butter for brushing the baking tin
Extra caster sugar for dredging over the baked shortbread
    while it is still hot

Brush the melted butter around the baking tray. Sieve the
flour, semolina (or ground rice) and caster sugar into a
mixing bowl. Cut the butter into the dry ingredients,
then rub in with your fingers (you can also do this in a
food processor) to combine to a dough. Press the shortbread dough evenly over the entire inside of the buttered
baking tray. Then with a fork make even rows of fork
pricks over the entire surface. Bake in a low oven (150°C
/ 300°F / gas 2) for about 1¼ hours. The shortbread
should be a pale golden colour and be shrinking in from

the sides of the tin slightly. Remove from the oven and dust with sieved caster sugar. After 10 minutes or so, cut the shortbread into even rectangles and then leave in the tin until cold. Store the cold shortbread in an airtight container.

Apple pancakes with cinnamon butter

Makes about 12 pancakes

220g (8oz) plain flour
1 tablespoon baking powder
50g (2oz) caster sugar
50g (2oz) butter, melted
2 large eggs, beaten
150ml (¼ pint) milk
2 good eating apples, peeled and cored

Sieve the flour, baking powder and sugar into a bowl. Beat the eggs with the milk, then add this mixture to the dry ingredients, along with the melted butter, and beat to a smooth, thick batter. Grate the apples into this. Meanwhile, heat a large griddle (you can use a sauté or frying pan instead) and rub it over with butter. Put spoonsful of batter, evenly and well spaced, onto the very hot griddle. When tiny bubbles form in each pancake, flip them over with a spatula to cook on their other side for about a minute. Lift them onto a rack and cover with a tea towel as you make up the remainder of the pancake batter.

For the cinnamon butter:
120g (4oz) soft butter
1 level teaspoon ground cinnamon
2 rounded tablespoons soft light brown sugar

Beat the butter, cinnamon and sugar together until very light and almost fluffy. Serve the pancakes just warm, with the cinnamon butter handed round separately.

Atholl brose

In restaurants and cafes all over Scotland you will find
Cranachan on the pudding menu. Cranachan is made by
adding fresh raspberries to the recipe below, which is a
heavenly concoction of whisky, honey, cream and toasted
pinhead oatmeal. I like to serve this in small glasses.

Serves 6
120g (4oz) pinhead oatmeal
450ml (¾ pint) double cream
4 tablespoons whisky of your choice
2 tablespoons honey of your choice (for me, this is never heather honey, which I personally find far too strong in flavour)

Start by toasting the pinhead oatmeal, as this needs to be allowed time to cool completely. Put the pinhead oatmeal into a dry frying or sauté pan over a moderately high heat. Shake the pan until the oatmeal turns a pale biscuit colour, about 4–5 minutes. Take the pan off the heat, tip the toasted pinhead oatmeal onto a plate to cool quickly. This is much better a way to 'toast' the oatmeal rather than putting it onto a baking tray under a grill or into an oven. It's all too easy to forget it, and scorch it.

Whip the cream with the whisky, but not too stiffly. Dip a tablespoon into a jug of very hot water for a minute, then spoon the honey into a saucepan. The honey will slip easily from the hot metal spoon. Warm the honey until it becomes runny. Cool slightly and then mix it into the whipped whisky cream – the cream should be sufficiently cold that the warm runny honey quickly cools on impact. Fold the cooled, toasted pinhead thoroughly through the whisky and honey cream, and divide evenly between 6 small glasses.

Variation

If you want to turn this into Cranachan, add 220g (8oz) fresh raspberries to the mixture. You will need slightly larger glasses!

Bramble and apple fudge oat crumble

This simple pudding has been a great favourite with my family and friends over the decades. It is delicious served with crème fraiche or vanilla ice cream – or both! I like to serve it warm, but it can be made 24 hours in advance and reheated gently before serving, and doesn't deteriorate at all. You can adjust the ratio of brambles to apples according to how many brambles you have. Picking brambles is a favourite occupation of mine during late summer/early autumn. But how many brambles ripen each year depends entirely on the weather – rain at the

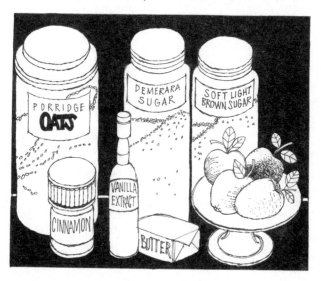

point when brambles turn from red to juicy black can destroy the crop for that year. But if the sun shines, and you pick a glut, remember that they freeze exceptionally well just packed into thick poly bags.

Serves 6
675g (1½ lb) brambles
4 good eating apples, peeled, cored and chopped
120g (4oz) soft light brown sugar

For the crumble:
220g (8oz) rolled (porridge) oats
120g (4oz) butter
120g (4oz) Demerara sugar
½ teaspoon vanilla extract
A small pinch ground cinnamon

Put the brambles, chopped apples and soft brown sugar into a saucepan. Put the lid on the pan and cook on a gentle heat, stirring the contents occasionally but always re-covering with the lid. The juices will gradually start to run from the brambles, and the sugar will dissolve. When the brambles are soft, take the pan off the heat and tip the contents into a wide, shallow ovenproof dish. Leave to cool.

Make the crumble by melting the butter in a wide-based pan, or a sauté pan, and add the Demerara sugar. Stir and cook for 3–4 minutes, adding the vanilla and cinnamon during this time. Then add the rolled oats, mixing thoroughly. Spoon the crumble evenly over the surface of the cooled bramble and apples. Bake in a moderate heat (180°C / 350°F / gas 4) for 35–40 minutes, or until the crumble is crispy and light brown in colour. Serve warm.

Iced whisky and honey creams

These iced creams have formed the pudding course for many a St Andrew's Day dinner – and any other special Scottish celebratory occasion. They are simple and quick to make, and exceptionally good to eat. The only caution I would give is not to use a heather honey, because it does have an overpowering taste. Which whisky you choose is up to you. (I use Grouse, because I do so love their advertisements!) The iced whisky and honey creams have to be made in advance so as to freeze, but because of their whisky content they never freeze rock solid, so they can be spooned straight from the freezer if you forget to bring them into the fridge half an hour ahead of serving them. I like to serve shortbread with these.

Serves 6
300ml (½ pint) double cream
4 tablespoons whisky
4 large egg yolks
4 level tablespoons honey

Whip the cream together with the whisky, but not too stiffly. Spoon the honey into a saucepan (dip the spoon into very hot water before and in between each spoonful – the honey slips easily from the spoon into the pan). Heat the honey until it is very hot. With a hand-held electric whisk, beat the egg yolks in a bowl, and add the

very hot honey in a thin, steady stream as you whisk.
Continue whisking until the mixture is greatly increased
in volume and is very thick and almost cold – about 5–7
minutes. When the egg and honey mixture is no hotter
than tepid, fold it and the whisky cream together
thoroughly. Divide evenly between 6 ramekins, cover
each with cling film, and freeze.

NB: Put the ramekins into the fridge about
half an hour before serving. Please avoid
using a sprig of mint
to garnish! A small
sprig of lavender
looks good, or
heather, in season.

Preserves

Lemon curd

This is one of the most delicious and versatile of preserves. You can substitute 4 Seville oranges for the 3 lemons during the all-too-brief marmalade orange season. You can use 3 limes instead of lemons, to make lime curd. The curd will keep for up to a week in the fridge, but it also freezes very well. Lemon curd is delicious eaten on warm scones, oatcakes, bread or toast, and it is also very good as a filling for a sponge cake, together with a layer of whipped cream. Or it can be folded into whipped cream and used to sandwich meringues together. Lemon curd is just so good, and people love being gifted with a pot of it!

_____

Makes one large pot
1 large egg beaten well with 2 large egg yolks
120g (4oz) caster sugar
120g (4oz) butter, cut into small bits
Finely grated rind of 3 lemons
Juice of 2 lemons (and remember that all citrus fruit yields so
    much more juice if the fruit are warm, at room temperature,
    rather than being chilled)

_____

Put a large jam jar into a low-temperature oven to warm. Put the sugar and butter into a Pyrex bowl with the beaten egg and yolks, and add the finely grated lemon rind and lemon juice. Put the bowl into a saucepan containing 6cm (2") simmering water, and stir the contents of the bowl, using a flat whisk, until the butter melts and the sugar dissolves. Slowly the curd starts to thicken over the heat. Stir occasionally until it is thick. Take the bowl off the heat and pour and scrape the curd from the bowl into the warmed jam jar. When cold, cover the jar with its lid and store the cooled curd in the fridge until required.

Marmalade

It is said that marmalade originated in the days of Mary, Queen of Scots. Whether this is true or not, I love to believe it. Marmalade is synonymous with Dundee, where Keiller's used to reign supreme in commercial marmalade making. These days, excellent marmalade is made by a number of companies, notably Mackays in Angus. But this is my marmalade recipe. I love it.

I like to make a series of batches of the following amount of fruit, which yields between 6 and 8 450g pots each session.

1.4kg (3lb) citrus fruit, to include 3 Seville oranges, the rest made
    up with sweet orange, lemon, lime, Clementine, pink grapefruit
450g (1lb) granulated or pectin-rich sugar per 600ml (1 pint)
    of juice and sliced or diced peel

Scrub the citrus fruit well under running hot water, to remove the preservative with which they are sprayed. Put the washed fruit, whole, into a jam pan or large pan, and add about 2.4 litres (4 pints) cold water. Cover the pan with its lid and put on heat until the water reaches a gentle simmer. Simmer gently for 2–3 hours, or until the peel feels tender when you stick a fork into one of the fruits. Take the pan off the heat and cool the contents.

On a board, cut the fruit in half and scrape the inside of each fruit into a small saucepan, pips and all. Add

600ml (1 pint) cold water, put this saucepan onto heat, bring the liquid to simmer and simmer for 10 minutes.

Meanwhile, finely slice or dice the peel of each citrus fruit. Put this back into the liquid in which they simmered. Strain the liquid from the small saucepan into the big pan. Measure this liquid, using a plastic measuring jug. Add 450g (1lb) sugar per 600ml (pint).

Put a tray of scrupulously clean jam jars into a low-temperature oven.

Put the jam pan on the heat and stir until you no longer feel any grittiness beneath your wooden spoon. Only then allow the marmalade to come to a fast, rolling boil.

Put a saucer into the fridge – this is for testing, 10 minutes after the boiling begins. Watch the jam pan like a hawk: beware over-boiling. As the bubbles start to become smaller, after about 10 minutes' fast boiling, draw the pan off the heat, and dribble about a teaspoon of marmalade onto the chilled saucer. Leave for several minutes, then gently push the surface of the dribble with your fingertip: if it wrinkles on the surface you have a 'set'. If it doesn't, put the jam pan back on the heat, boil fast for a few more minutes, then repeat the test, but be sure to draw the jam pan off the heat during the testing.

The quicker the set is achieved, the brighter and fresher will be the appearance of the marmalade. Pour into the warmed jars, cover each with a waxed disc, cool, then seal each jar with a disc of cellophane. Label, and store on shelves in a cool place, ideally a larder.

MARIE
REINE
D'ESCOS

Jam
SUGAR

Rowan & Apple
AUTUMN 2015

CINNAMON
STICK

Rowan and apple jelly

Rowan trees are glorious in the autumn, with their bright orange berries and their copper-coloured leaves. Rowan jelly is so good with all game and venison, but rowan berries are bitter, so I add eating apples to my jelly to soften the flavour. The cinnamon stick gives a hint of spice to the jelly, too.

Makes about six 450g (1lb) jars

900g (2lb) rowan berries, stripped from their stalks
900g (2lb) good eating apples, quartered – skin and seeds and all
2.5 litres (4 pints) water
1 cinnamon stick
450g (1lb) granulated or pectin-rich sugar per 600ml (1 pint) liquid

---

Put 6–8 scrupulously clean jam jars on a baking tray in a low-temperature oven, to heat through.

Put the berries, quartered apples, cinnamon stick and water into a large pan. Put this on the heat and bring the liquid to a gentle simmer. Cover the pan with its lid and simmer the contents gently for 35–40 minutes, or until the berries are squishable when pressed against the sides of the pan with the back of a wooden spoon. Take the pan off the heat. Strain the contents through a fine-meshed sieve into measure jugs or a very large bowl.

Measure the strained liquid into the rinsed-out large pan, and add 450g (1lb) granulated sugar for each 600ml

(1 pint) of liquid. Over heat, stir until there is no longer the gritty feeling from undissolved sugar. Then bring the contents of the pan to a fast rolling boil. Put a saucer in the fridge to chill, ready for testing to see if the jelly has reached a 'set'.

After 10 minutes' fast boiling, draw the pan off the heat and put a dribble of the liquid onto the chilled saucer. Leave for several minutes before gently pushing the surface of the dribble with your fingertip – if the jelly wrinkles, you have achieved a set. If it doesn't wrinkle, put the pan back on the heat and bring the liquid back to boiling point. Boil fast for a further few minutes before repeating the setting test.

Pot into the warmed jars, put a waxed paper disc on top of each, leave to cool before sealing with cellophane discs. Label the pots and store in a cool place, ideally a larder.

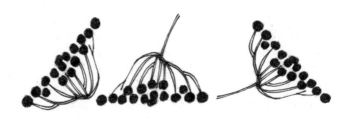

CINNAMON
STICK